# AFTERNOON HORSES

# Afternoon Horses

Deirdre Kessler

Acorn Press
Charlottetown
2009

Cover image: *Fireweed Trail* (detail) by Cecily Donnelly
Editing by Gillian Robinson
Design by Matthew MacKay
Printing in Canada by Hignell Book Printing

The publisher acknowledges the support of the Government of Canada through the Book Publishing Industry Development Program (BPIDP) of the Department of Canadian Heritage for our publishing activities. We also acknowledge the support of the Canada Council for the Arts and the Prince Edward Island Department of Communities, Cultural Affairs, and Labour for our publishing program.

Library and Archives Canada Cataloguing in Publication

Kessler, Deirdre
        Afternoon horses / Deirdre Kessler.
Poems.
ISBN 978-1-894838-39-9
        I. Title.
PS8571.E77A68 2009        C811'.54        C2009-904417-X

**ACORNPRESS**
P.O. Box 22024
Charlottetown, Prince Edward Island
C1A 9J2

**acornpresscanada.com**

To John Smith,
with love and thanks for decades
of conversation and education about poetry,
and to my superb circle of family,
with much love.

# CONTENTS

In other states:
Tasmania, Guerrero, Oregon

### Soundings

A retreat to middle distance,
then out, away, until—
there: a patch of wilderness
on a distant continent, or

the ridgetop coyote trail
my feet came to know by day,
by night; and the spring

buried in a mesquite thicket;
no matter the scratches on entry—
the water, the water.

And you, horses, in a fold of prairie,
sere grasses hiding new growth;

and you, cetaceans, travelling
half the globe to winter home.

In the deep channel, you tune
to family across the expanse,
respond: we're here, on our way;
we're alive.

I cast out, and this moment,
somewhere, you are safe.

### Franklin on the Huon River, Tasmania, spring

I could linger on the shore of you,
like this bit of willow fluff
swirled sunward, a late-October
afternoon, to land somewhere,
take root.

See that little place
nestled halfway up a Huon slope?
Spring-green, steep, and, there—
the cluster of eucalypts,
a level niche where a whaler
built a stone cottage for a local girl,
and river, eastern shore, mountain
satisfied his longing for a distant horizon.

He built seagoing vessels for others,
came home at night, planted apple trees,
raised a few head of cattle and children.

The century moved along;
the grandchildren grew old,
sold the place to a neighbour;
now the neighbour's niece is looking
for a good price: *Quaint, historic
cottage with an unfiltered view.*

That's how it goes, doesn't it?
Sometimes we linger; other times
the hillside stays inside us,
and the river, and the dark
sleeping beauties of mountains.

*Etched in the capstone of the east gate column*
*at the top of Kelly Steps in Hobart, Tasmania:*
KELLY STREET
JANUARY 1840
J.K.

## Kelly Steps

Footfall makes the first sixteen ring,
echo against the high walls.
And there's a resonance
with a hollow below,
where the original ones sheltered
from a squall, perhaps, or left a cache
of hunting gear; where lichens still do
their slow compositions in stone,
negotiating with southwind
and salt.

Blocks of sandstone, yellow ochre
and grey, quarried from this cliff,
engineered to three tiers:
sixteen wide steps, then a landing
and right-angle turn to west—Mt. Wellington
a surprise each climb;
earlier cloud-shrouded, now not;
then fifteen steps, landing,
turn back south;
sixteen more.

The River Derwent carved its own deep way,
long before Captain James Kelly pointed,
said, "Steps here," and his second mate
rounded up a crew of locals,
drove them, paid them badly
in the end.

The language of stone shifts
to meet the quarryman, suits the carver
and the chisel; rock remembers rope
and sweat, grain by grain weeps
for families sundered, whales
slaughtered, until
surface sorrow erodes,
is windsown elsewhere.

The foot finds the worn places,
scuffed with lives
ascending,
        descending.

### Collateral damage

Words shaped like joeys
tumble out of your mouth,
strange, gentle sounds
born of your red earth.

The soft-eyed deer of my continent
have no pouches for caching
small versions of themselves.

A moment before you step,
you hesitate. This, on another day,
in a land-mined desert far from here.
A skin shed with each outing and return.

Then, the expected shock,
and your mate has opened out
in ways you cannot fix.
Rest, you tell him, rest.

You cover him with words
and jacket until he dies,
maybe lives. Either way, you

backtrack, each step present tense,
each breath nothing more,
nothing less.

A bullet has little chance
of piercing the offspring
if aimed at the mother's heart.
The joey lives a while.
The pouch grows cold.

### Indian summer

Between known and nameless,
a liminal season. Pause to breathe,
move through the days at a lope, easy.

Recollections of full-blooded summer,
legs wrapped around the motorcycle,
hypnotic red earth and horizon unbound,
face welcoming the desert wind.

Pit stops where once the aborigines' paths
converged before the invention of time;
now a hardy couple sell shade, beer, salty
meat; on a radio, loud music from the coasts.

Hidden Springs Motel behind the store,
plywood walls and curtains on a string.
The short-term help always beautiful,
young women and men far from home and happy.

Halfway out of the world, this season.
Ahead, an edge to ride, but here, bittersweet
recollection buffered by an indolent sky.

Sweet mornings, each a slow breath of a world
remembering how the hands find the right places
in dark rooms or under stars in the middle of nowhere,
in the middle of the night.

## *Paperweight*

No soapflakes here
to swirl around a cheesy
winterscape, but amber,
the weight comforting
in the palm.

Each gesture and phrase fixed
in the golden resin; blue
at the top of Mt. Wellington;
clouds distant down the valley,
gathering and sundering over
the South Ocean.

Smoothed by the Roaring Forties
and ten thousand hands, a grey rail
angles along the boardwalk
to the lookout point. Below,
the rock-strewn field
Darwin clambered over,
and a flame-breasted robin.

Later, rain and rain and rain
while Coyote Serenade plays
under a canopy outside
Longley International Pub,
no one but me from farther away
than neighbouring hillside farms,
or Hobart, and you,
a temporary resident
from nowhere and everywhere,
hard to pin down a place
you'd call home.

All this inside, caught—
though anyone can see the cracks,
places where the sap oozes, spreads out,
and a creature emerges, shakes
its wings, lets the sun dry up droplets
of millennia-old transpiration,
takes flight.

### Children of the Poet-king
*for Judy Gaudet*

Netzahualcoyotl children in the coastal village,
language still in the Texcoco hills, your ears
must tune to Spanish, tongues must enter
a new world; you speak mountain
and stream, path to high field.

Your father and uncles gone a year,
seeking work, so you and mama followed
from high village to lower one,
then a bus to Zihuatanejo,
mama's sister there already;
your father, too. Perhaps.
Someone had a letter from Zihua.

You sold Chiclets on the streets
until a teacher from the Netza School
found you, spoke your ancient words,
brought you here, a place for you and mama
to sleep, eat. New clothes and others
from villages near yours, all of you
learning *escuela, gracias, señora.*

We meet, speak one word,
our sandaled feet close
on sun-soaked, dusty ground,
bougainvillea climbing the wall
behind you, soft sea air
embracing us both.
Holà.

### The same water

One touchstone this duration
has been a Collins Spanish Grammar.
Every day or so a recitation,
rules and examples. And I read Neruda,
aloud, in Spanish, stopping to wonder
or weep, mull or drift
before looking at the English versions.

*Yo escribi cinco versos:*
*uno verde,*
*otro era un pan redondo...*

How much Spanish does one need to know
to understand the writing of five poems,
one green, another a loaf of round bread...

Collins informs me in a boxed item on nouns, p. 6:
*Days of the week and months of the year are masculine,*
*so are languages, mountains, and seas.*

There is no such boxed item about feminine nouns.
Two pages farther on, though:
*la canción*
*la luz.*

Song and light and water and axe are feminine.

*La misma agua*, the example.

Yes, I think, the same water,
it is all the same water.
The same light, the same song,

the same small handaxe,
like the one by my woodstove,
the one I take camping,

the axe that crosses continents
and never transmutes to a gun
or to an experiment in the seas
in Mururoa Atoll.

### Stinkingwater Pass

Close to our destination now,
after miles of winding,
bending to the Malheur River,
curving with road and river.

We overtake a truck going up
towards the pass,
the only traffic in miles,
flatbed stacked with I-beams
and struts.
The load slows the truck
until we are both
in our lowest gears.
Politely the trucker
makes space for us,
pulls to the shoulder,
lets us cruise by
as we go towards the summit.

We wave at the trucker,
see his dashboard stocked
with stuffed toys,
objects dangling
from the visors.
Wonder how he sees the road.

Through the pass we come,
and the world changes.
We pause at the pivot point,
though the car hurtles us
downward into the Great Basin.

We're on our way
to Malheur Field Station.
We've got our struts,
got our I-beams.

### Edge of Malheur Desert

At Stinkingwater Pass, elevation 4848',
we enter this great basin for the first time,
and know from coral-pink sun, eye-level,
bank of blue-grey clouds,

know from zoomed retreat of horizon,
from antelope,
      white pelican,
           great horned owl,
black-eared jackrabbit,
dome of half-lit sky,
      water
           everywhere close to the surface,

know we have arrived
at the great reckoning place,
plateau between the ranges
where western rivers were born.

      No echoes here.
We say hello and the sound
         spreads out,
           water on a plate.
Bold and swift as nighthawks,
we have landed.

*Malheur Field Station*
*Harney County, Oregon*
*August 2001*

### On the road to Krumbo Reservoir, Oregon
*for Ursula Le Guin*

Strung like beads along the road
on the way to Krumbo,
you and I and all of us.
Someone leads us to it,
the rock the People etched.

Strung like beads along a dusty path,
cattle on the way to Krumbo:
brindle mother, brindle baby,
Hereford cow and two red calves,
another roan and her roan monthling,
a final cow, white-faced, with twins.

Cattle single file on the sunken trail,
mid-morning towards the wetlands.
South to the caged-rock corner,
through the gap and up along,
follow the curve of pallisades,
tumbled blocks, long grass, longer;
wetter now, a downslope and
the path forks: one branch goes
towards Jack's Mountain,
the other to reeds and mud and lake,
marsh grass to the babies' muzzles.

Strung like beads along the road
on the way to Krumbo,
brindle mother, brindle baby,
you and I and all of us.
Someone leads us to it—
the rock the People etched.

Blueberries in a green bowl

### The names of things

He's four now, puts on
his own little clothes, speaks
in complete sentences, tells me
he lives in Toronto, Ontario, Canada,
and has been to many places:
Prince Edwer Dyelan,
Nova Scotia, and the zoo.

What do you see at the zoo?

*Giraffes and lions and afternoon horses.*

He is eating blueberries
picked the day before in a field
above dyked marshlands,
Annapolis Valley highbush berries,
the flock of family browsing
in the same reverie.

And what are afternoon horses?

*They go places in the afternoon.*

That's how it is with the world,
the names of things.
Blueberries in a green bowl.
A child on his knees on a chair
eating with a big spoon,
discussing life.

### Planet Venus

In his eighth month, an odd little fellow,
he remembers all the way from morning
that I'd told him if the night were clear,
not too cloudy, we could go outside
when it is dark to look for the moon.

*See moon*, he says before bedtime.

We stand on the deck
in squeaking, sharp February cold,
looking into as much night sky
as a city can muster.
He is in pajamas, wrapped
in a blanket, in my arms.
There is the moon, nearly full.

*Moon! Moon!*

In the closer distance,
the whistle of a train.

"Listen: a train whistle."

*Train.*

And then I see Venus,
high in the southeast, gasp:
"Planet Venus, far, far away!"
He looks where I point, sees it.

*Planet Venus! Planet Venus!*

This year Venus is as bright
as when van Gogh painted
*House on Remy Street*, 1889.

A *Scientific American* writer tracked Venus
back to Vincent's nights in Arles.
It wasn't lunacy; it was the nearness
and brightness of Venus
that drove him beauty-mad that time.

The child is spellbound;
I am cold. We come inside.
He tells the story to his mother.

*Moon. Not too cloudy. Train.*
*Far away. Planet Venus!*

### Siblings

Her brother calculates the moment,
lays out the plan, whispers:

*Firtht I will go acroth the room.*
*Then I will pinth Thayth.*

His infant tongue cannot navigate
the esses, but we understand:

*First I will go across the room.*
*Then I will pinch Chase.*

He sets out from the block tower
he has constructed with sure, small hands.
But we have learned how he plots revenge
on his baby sister, and we listen closely
to his *sotto voce* strategies.

"It's not nice to pinch people," we say.

Our opposition adds force
to his pigeon-toed shuffle
across the hardwood.

Foiled when we scoop her up,
he diverts to the new upholstered chair,
wipes his nose on it, says,

*It'th not nith to thnot people.*

He has been told not to wipe
a snotty nose on people and chairs.

Satisfied, the master builder
returns to his tower of blocks.

When she's old enough to talk,
Chase can warn us, screams
at the first whisper of intent,
the slightest touch.

She doesn't bother learning letters;
he reads everything, always did—
she learns things unwritten.

He loves his mother the way calf loves cow;
a baby chimp never wanting to be separate,
always an arm holding on,
a foot keeping contact.

How could she do this to him.

At five he asks his mother how old
he needs to be to marry.
She hesitates. Well,
eighteen or twenty. Why?

He wants to marry her.

Another day, he asks when she will die.
Not for a long, long time.

*When will I die?*
Not for a long, long, *long* time.

Chase listens, says nothing.

Three days later on the Danforth,
at a Japanese restaurant,
Chase is insistent, "Mom. MOM!"
*When do I get back from dying?*

### Laugh in the drawer

Chase was cut out of her mother,
wrapped up, taken screaming, clutching,
down the hall to the neonatal room,
the arrow of shriek piercing walls,
slipping under doors, seeking the other,
the rest of her, the mother, solace.

The mother, exhausted from hours
of unfruitful labour, the sudden
decision to slit her open—
a nightmare those first forty-eight hours.
Ever since, the child wakes in the night,
cries.

When she found the word *monster,*
she used it. Monsters in the dreams,
in the room, in the night.

*Once I heard a laugh in my pillow,*
she tells me. She's four now,
a feisty girl who cannot be forced
against her will. It is impossible
to carry her away from the swings,
upstairs to bed, out the door.
She can disconnect her arms
from her shoulders, wriggle, slither,
a mass of muscle and intent.

Lately, Chase goes nowhere without
her shrine—a montage of stickers,
small drawings of Dora the Explorer
pasted on a piece of construction paper
that can be folded like a card,
carried in the Dora backpack.

*I heard something in my pillow—*
*a laugh—and there was a face*
*under my pillow.*

She likes the story about her brother's
imaginary devil-girl, a mean child
named Poonan who came from his dreams
when he was a year and a half old.

Poonan pinches people, laughs,
runs away. Poonan is jealous
and pushy and has no manners.

*And once I heard a laugh in my drawer,*
*and it was Poonan.*
*I never want to see her again!*

### Dusky seaside sparrow

*Read four stories,* she says.

It's late: two stories.

*No, four.*

You need sleep, little girl.
Two stories tonight.

*Three stories.*

Two.

*But will you lie with me a while?*

After the stories, she needs stories.
Always a winding down from the day with this child,
rituals to calm, to prepare her
for being left alone with night demons.

*Don't go yet.*

I must go now.
It is time for you to sleep.

Her eyelids are heavy.
It won't be long until she crashes,
the transition infinitesimal.
I begin to extricate myself from her side.

Her eyes fly wide.
She sits up, fully awake, asks:

*Who will be the last baby in the world?*

## Epiphany

But what I meant to say was my brother phoned.
He was in his car, en route from seeing a friend
north of the Golden Gate, in Marin County,
and had crossed the Richmond Bridge,
was heading south on the bay side.

"I had an epiphany this morning," he says.

After years of ignoring them, working
his engineer job, good at whatever he does,
a musician who often carries a length of rope
for dull moments, making knots, complicated ones,
from books, his fingers doing the same kind of thing
on his mandolin, only without instruction—
after decades of disregarding his demons,
he has turned and is staring into the undergrowth,
daring them to come out, occasionally giving chase.

I am delighted, imagine a number of revelations
my brother might have had. What?

"I have too many shirts.

"I must have sixty-five shirts.
Too many, too much choice.
If I didn't have so many shirts,
I think my life would be clear."

### Hands
*for Cecily*

It's how you measure a horse, you say.
We are standing by black-maned Softy,
one brown patch on his back
exactly like a saddle,
and he so interested in us.

You give me a knee up.
Thirteen hands two. To his withers.
These are his withers, you say.
I know the word from books.

I've ridden an imaginary horse for years;
some days I barely dismount.
In dreams a herd, and I choose a black horse,
or white, bay, pinto, roan, grey—I can
never decide which colour I like best
until I see Softy.

You know how to hold the reins, ride bareback
or with saddle, groom, pick out the hooves.
Your hands move to quiet Softy
when he gets too playful for a seven-year-old,
hands that know far more than the year and a half
you've lived longer than I have.

We're two little girls riding bareback,
living inside the same script: pony express,
bandits, circus. The dialogue from books
or made up on the spot, rehearsed
as we shoot one another off Softy,
lie dead on the ground, say:
No, let's do it again, only this time, you...

Now, your hands hold paintbrushes,
oil crayons, shovel, fencing tools,
computer mouse, chainsaw.

Or you lift the saddle from its rack
and into the station wagon, drive
three hundred miles to ride with a friend.

I think: look at her, the beauty,
how she moves in the world with those hands,
caressing the nervous dog, fixing the roof,
or fetching arugula from the garden.

### Walking stick

Always the slap of screendoor as we race outside.
Free again! Everything available at once: sky, sun,
grass, our dog Stuffy, Honeydripper, the Jersey cow,
hens, honeysuckle, mulberries, blackberries, and
sometimes—what is it?

In shadows behind the barn, where things were abandoned
by people who had lived in our house, kept their own hens
and cows in our barn: worn leather harness, a harrow,
empty tins of Prince Albert tobacco, red-painted
labels still vibrant, lids rusted shut.

My older brother said to the storekeeper
at Five Points Junction Variety down the road:
Do you have Prince Albert in a can?
How we dissolved in laughter outside the store,
choking out the punchline over and over:
"Then you'd better let him out. He might suffocate!"

There in the low branches something transforms
from a stick to something else.
It has a head.
It has eyes!

Already so much of life surprises,
every outing something bright and new.
The creature stops. Again it is a stick.
How is such a thing possible?

### Time

In this dream
I am telling you
time is half an orange,
squeezed,
turned inside out
like a cap.
Mornings, we'd wait
by our mother's
orange juice
presser, wait
for our half,
turn it inside out,
clean it bare,
fruit pulp hanging
from the edges
doubly sweet.
Every time,
the membrane
pulls away cleanly,
subcutaneous layer
astringent, thrilling.
The perfection of it all.

### Midnight at the oasis

I am five and these things
fit together: Brer Rabbit
and the Tarbaby—
poor Brer Rabbit
kicking that rude Tarbaby,
getting his furry self
all stuck in the tar.

We live next door
to a highways storage yard:
heaps of sand and cinders
for winter and a wall
of stacked cans of tar
for patching summer roads.
Perfect, sun-warmed tar
spilled on concrete,
bubbling up,
cooling down at night.
Dribbles and globs.
Half-used cans with lids askew.

We roll that tar
round ball,
round ball
in our little hands,
push it with the toes
of our sneakers.
I eat some—the seductive
temperature and texture
between my fingers,
then tar in my mouth
and I understand
how touch and taste
are different.

Tar and Brer Fox's trick
on Brer Rabbit are rolled together
with one more thing:
sure knowledge of how to escape.

Brer Rabbit tells Brer Fox,
"Oh, whatever you do,
jes' doan throw me
in dat briarpatch!"

What does Brer Fox do?
He pitches that rabbit
into that briarpatch.
Yes, Brer Rabbit lands
smack-dab in the middle
of his briary home.

~

I am tenting in an oasis
in Death Valley,
thirty years later.
Shade from desert sun
in the cool of willows
along a creek
my escape
from winter in
Prince Edward Island.

Tent, birdbook, journal.
I am happy.
Mornings I jog;
afternoons I hike ten kilometres
to a mineral spring;
nights, there's dancing
at a rough bar,
but I slip out the back door
before the ugly stuff starts.

No one knows who I am
or where I camp.
That's what I think.
This night, I doze under stars
on a flat rock by my campfire
a distance from the hidden tent.

Midnight at the oasis.

Then they come roaring
into the canyon in pickup trucks,
gun engines up the rutted track
towards the creek.

I am standing, kicking sand
over the coals, running
back towards the tent, see
how easily found
a northern girl is;
how obvious the campsite;
how clear from months of sidelong
scrutiny at the bar
what is about to unfold.

But I remember a story.
I know this thatch
of willow and salt cedar,
creosote bush and mesquite.
I grab my pack from the tent:
passport, wallet, journal, water bottle.
I creep into the thicket, keep going,
push with my soft-skinned hands and face
through the underbrush;
crouch, crawl—and now
I am home.
Smack-dab in the middle.

### Light from the hallway

Later she tells me I was a good baby, so good,
neighbours did not know I was there.
We live on Long Lane, our house attached to others
like a train curving down a slope of city.
Neighbours know my curly-haired brother,
two-and-a-half when I come home from the hospital
with his mother. And they know my sister,
eleven, the one, they whisper,
who has a different father and maybe
the father of curly-head does not like her.

I am six months old, asleep in an almost-dark room.
Everything is familiar—every night the narrow path
of light falls across the floor the same way
and goes the same way up the wall.
My eyes are heavy, too heavy to keep her by me.
Sleep steals me, almost carries me away.
I see her retreat, light widening, narrowing
to the familiar pattern across the floor, up the wall.
She is never far away. I am happy. I let go.

Now I cry awake. My arm, my leg—I roll away
from the pain, pull myself to hands and knees.
A growl. Growling. I stare through the slats.
There is nothing but the terrifying sound.
Something behind me grabs my leg, holds on.
I shriek. The door opens to light and closes again,
but she is not here. Again I wail, and she appears,
sweeps me to her arms, comforts me, rocks me.

Sleep is irresistible, but the next night,
when she retreats, my eyes stay open.
The swath of light widens, closes.
The growl, the pincer, the shriek. The light
widens, closes. She does not come. Then the room
fills with light. She sweeps me up, presses me close.
She stays longer the next night, sings,
leaves the door wide open. I sleep.

"I am a lion. I am going to eat you."
Only tone and pain do I understand. Not words.
It grabs and holds my side, twists the flesh.
Before I can scramble away, the overhead light
is on and my mother has grabbed the monster
under the crib, pulled him out. She turns her voice
hard to him. "You may not do this. She is a baby.
You may not scare her or hurt her. Do you understand?"
His face contorts. He cries. That beautiful head nods;
curls of an angel. How has he fallen so far from grace?
She picks me up, comforts me, tells me there is
no monster, nothing to fear. He is sorry. All is well.

I understand relief in her voice: the good baby
crying for no reason. We walk him together
to his room, see him into his bed, covered.
And I have learned something: how to sleep
in the middle of my crib, exactly in the middle,
where no monster can grab ahold of my fat little self.
And I have learned how to raise the living with a scream.
Later, my brother apologizes. He is thirty
and has a curly-haired baby of his own, one
who likes the light left on when he sleeps.

### Push or pull?

Back of the Kastenbaum house
on Providence Road—the same road
George Washington took from the capital
to Valley Forge two centuries ago,
then a wagon track that rumbled
with supplies for cold young men at war—
back of Jerry Kastenbaum's, a wood
with small-trunked trees, a sumac grove,
filtered light welcome
in a Pennsylvania summer.

My brother Pete and Jerry Kastenbaum
are big boys, but let the little sister
tag along today. We follow a path
that winds to the creek.

I've been there by myself, seeking
the green gloom and solace of crayfish.
Underwater, a crayfish scuttles, buries itself,
the fine sand quickly filling the hole—
mesmerizing, like our mama's eggtimer.
How does it do that? One grain at a time,
fast, steady. Gone. Crayfish safe.

We never kill them anyway.
Pete and Jerry aren't cruel boys.
Jerry's brother Mikey has a lisp.
*Puth or pull?* he asks when it's my turn
in the red Radio Flyer.
Hard to say which is more thrilling:
to be pushed or pulled
in a wagon by a big boy.

We duck and whisper on the trail.
Mama's been reading us James Fenimore Cooper
evenings at the round mahogany table.
Pete is the trailblazer.
We come to swamp cabbage.

I am never sure about the alien-sized
leaves growing out of black mud,
menacing. It is possible
the plants hide quicksand,
like Saturday matinées,
the good cowboy saved
by his lariat and trusty horse.

Pete and Jerry round a bend
and see the snake first,
twined in thin branches, eye-level.
Whoever saw a snake in a tree?

*Get something to put it in,*
Pete tells Jerry, and Jerry gallops
back along the trail.

My brother and I stare
into the snake's eyes,
fix it in the branches,
keep it from sliding away.

Why is Jerry taking such a long time?
Pete and I are puzzled.
Then we hear his awkward lope,
hard breath. Jerry appears,
holds out an old kettle,
spout too narrow for the snake,
lid rusted shut.

I understand for the first time
that our thoughts are different.
Not Pete's and mine,
but Jerry's and ours.

It isn't funny then, but later
we remember Jerry Kastenbaum
and the kettle and the snake.
Do we push or pull?

## Subtracting by seventeen

**A note about Brood X cicadas:**
*The emergence of Brood X (Ten) cicadas is a once-a-generation phenomenon. These creatures spend seventeen years underground in tunnels, sucking on tree roots for sustenance. When they emerge from the ground, they gather in trees in large, chorusing group-ings; the males sing, the females respond by flicking their wings; the males move closer and mating ensues. The females lay 400–600 eggs, and both adults die in a few weeks. When the eggs hatch, the young fall onto the ground, make their way to the base of grasses to feed for a while, then they burrow half a metre underground. And there they stay for seventeen years. The most recent emergence of Brood X was in May 2004.*


I.
They were everywhere, the husks,
and everywhere the singing.
We roamed the property,
adrenaline pumping,
plucking cicada shells
from the bark of trees,
awed. We didn't know that Brood Ten
would mark that May—the last year
we were all together, the last year
for the looped driveway, rampant
yellow roses at the centre
of the oval, dividing the sky
into blue and Vincent yellow
until our father hacked
the roses knee-high.

II.
It was the last year
of a wisteria-laden trellis
at the kitchen corner of the house,
two half walls of windows in winter,
screens in summer, horizontal lines
of bamboo filtering the afternoons.
Along the outside, a ledge
where the toad appeared evenings.

Mornings, bamboo rolled to top
and sweet purple air on our faces,
breakfast of scrambolies and whole wheat
toast, orange juice, squeezed
from the little tower of a presser,
Mama letting each of us
have an inverted orange cap
to strip clean after the pressing,
nothing wasted.

III.
It was the last year of Smokey,
the cat who loved our mother, met her
as she'd return from mailbox,
walk to town, design work now and then,
Chicago or New York.
Mama's home! with presents:
a peepshow Cinderella book,
a new feather pillow.

The last year for the barnyard chickens,
pets—how we loved the way they hunched
to be stroked, picked up; how they huddled
in their cubbies, undersides soft,
warm as a dream on the backs
of our little hands when reached in under
for eggs. Excuse me, Mrs. Hen, and thanks.

IV.
It was the last time the pattern
matched what we read at Sandy Bank School,
the *Dick and Jane* blueprint of parents,
house, family, dog. Our dog Stuffy,
Stuffy, my heart—brown eyebrows
on black fur lifting and settling
when we looked at each other;
brown paw up. Shake, Stuffy. Good boy.
He was wolf, lion, bear—whatever
he needed to be for the game. And wolf
on his own with the chickens. We learned

to keep the gate closed, our father's fury
worse than the dead hen, Stuffy's yelp
in my ears still.

V.
And I learned to stand between them.
Stuffy's chance to slink away. And, oh,
the freedom the moment I turned,
ran away myself, around the house,
the father chasing, slowed by split
attention, removing his belt
for the strapping,
giving my six-year-old legs
a moment's advantage, time enough
to leave the safety of dooryard, barnyard;
to dip under the electric fence, across
a field where neighbours kept a mule.
Running, laughing over my shoulder
to see him stop by the mulberry tree,
turn back towards the house,
shaking his head, anger spent, slow
recognition of the skinny child
in flight, his daughter, himself.

I could spend forever outside—that season,
no mulberries, but enough onion grass
and blue sky to sustain me forever.

VI.
Mama pointed out the cicadas
that had exited from the split
on the back of our treasures.
*Nymph cases*, she said, and let us
bring our collections indoors,
never shrieked, recoiled; let us
make mud pies, strip to underpants
to play in puddles warm
with an afternoon's rain.

Held us back behind the screen door
only until lightning and thunder moved on;
released us to flap outside,
three little kids, two, four, six.

VII.
Then, the year of Brood Ten,
three kids, five, seven, nine.
The last year in the grey
farmhouse at the edge of town,
now a cloverleaf where a highway
cuts through yellow rose,
mulberry tree, chicken coop.
House and wisteria gone—seedpods
still in our mother's possession
when she died, in the tray
with gum eraser, sandpaper,
Exacto knife—tools
of her drafting trade.

VIII.
We have them now, the seedpods,
waiting to plant them, waiting
for something. Brood Ten, maybe.
Imagine—seventeen years—long before
we were born, Brood Ten cicadas
in tunnels below the ground, sucking
on our mulberry tree roots, molting,
moving closer to the surface.

All that time underground and then
the trees thick with their singing,
the males buzzing, shrilling the sky,
females vibrating newly dried wings.

IX.
All for us, we thought, all for us
this thrill of life everywhere,
husks of cicada, six sharp legs

clinging to bark after the being
had detached, flown. Hens squatting,
warm eggs underneath. Silky
mud for us to roll in, laugh.
Stuffy circling, protecting, one eye
on us, one eye on the hens.
The father and mother playing
*Dick and Jane* today, no need
to run, to worry.

X.
It was a Brood Ten day.
We had no idea it would ever end.
No idea it was so long in the making.

Rearranging the sky

### Tethered to the moon

I have rearranged the sky
for you. Red stars over there,
a cluster of pomegranate seeds
to burst on your tongue.

Black holes on the ground level,
easy access to the parking garage.
And here, all your favourites
tethered to the moon like kites:
Leo, Lyra, horsehead nebula.

And I've nested the dippers,
small bear inside the great;
how they've longed for this.

The tricky part was calming
solar winds as they found
their interstellar cousins—
the termination shock
would have upset the arrangement,
made us fall apart again.

Remember when we walked away,
opposite directions,
nothing in its proper place.

### Alchemy

Was it just before
you closed the door behind you,
or did I close it?
Remember how the leaving was sustained
from room to room, circles widening
until there was no further we could go
and still be saying good-bye.

We were redrawing the boundaries then,
a sharp line around you,
head angling towards another life,
a curved line around me,
heart unable to catch up. Wait!

Just before the parting,
did an alchemist turn from his gold
to heat a crucible of amber,
warm the resin, melt those slow juices.

Could an alchemist with a careful hand
tip such a substance into our lives?
Could it ooze, seductive and comforting,
capture us, embrace us perfectly,
our bodies together for the first time,
hillocks and sap, suckle and clasp,
golden inside the fossil resin.

### Afternoon with van Gogh

A day like today, soft, warm,
summer lingering into November,
rose leaves scarlet, burnished by frost,
umber ferns, fragrant, still erect,
Vincent-yellow field grasses
strong with the arc of August,
and blue cirrus-whisked sky.
I breathe air too pure
to sustain any thought but this: you,
my landscape, you,
the colour of home.

### Now there is snow

Now there is snow
covering all these stalks,
snow to shroud blood
of nightshade berry,
hide rosette of mullein,
its woolly green leaves
clinging tight to the earth
by the side of the trail.

Under the snow,
October,
November
lie measured in footsteps.
Each step imprinted with you:
an angle of cheek, a sidelong look.

For now, let this all
be covered with snow,
let it rest for the winter.
In spring, we'll have forgotten
where each other is,
forgotten umber and vermilion
and midnight rattle of poplar leaves.

We will forget, the way a coyote
ignores a cache of rabbit,
hibernal bear neglects a salmon creek,
the way caribou lose the southland
in summer, the north in winter,
the way, at a whisper of wind, a lynx
shuns the cave where her kits lie curled,
hushed, hungry.

We're safe as silence,
cave entrance brush-covered,
a single set of tracks leading away,
no scent, no presence, safe
under white-quiet blanket of waiting,
feathery as forgetfulness.

### Winter deepens

Winter deepens overnight.
Earth-bundled worms nestle
beneath daylily or lupin,
violet or crocus,
It's too late to move the irises,
too late to rake one last time.

Here, finally, a clear marker
between now and that Indian summer night,
between now and you, striding
as though you knew the territory,
knew this town.

Your arms swing free;
no one waits for you.
Far from home you settle to yourself,
acknowledge this was what you had in mind
all along, this is the way you walk,
this is the way you remember Alberta,
cabin by creek, mockingbird welcome.

You wade to the middle of a stream,
cast, let the line drift
on the surface. Cast again.

And then dust on the backroads so thick,
you and your best friend
laugh yourselves silly.
First glimpse of prairie
when you leave the woods, drive to town:
sky as big as your dreams.

### Divided sky

This winter blue morning
bare branches divide the sky
rub their limbs past one another
in a sunrise stirring of wind.
I withdraw from sleep
to angles of cerulean,
irregular trapezoids.

My hands search, feel your traces
between my legs, but it's too late.
You've fled our only sanctuary.
I would follow, though the waking route
holds danger—through branches,
over the peak of neighbouring house,
higher, over the slumbered city,
across the freezing strait, still blue,
edges thickening against the shore.

I would migrate south, match patterns
of land and inlet against memory.
Measure marsh and open sea by heartbeats.
Shun insatiable strands of concrete
until—there, at last!

The grass-fringed bay rich and warm,
shallow waters everywhere.
There would be a perilous entry
through your yard, and you,
asleep, would you feel a sudden chill,
turn for warmth to someone close,
gather her sleeping towards you.

### *Winter settles into bone*

Winter settles into bone.
I wither to the back of the cave.
There's cable television
and a car that starts.
In the yard, splitting block,
neat stack of seasoned wood.
My axe cleaves spruce and birch.
Frost has permeated the core,
makes it easy for us to fall apart.
Wind pushes one old maple until it creaks;
or is the voice from elsewhere?
My eyes sweep the sky,
search branches for a clue.
But the wind plays tricks with direction,
the cry from farther away.
Yesterday, a cold so deep in central Mexico
monarch butterflies let go their hold,
fell sleeping, frozen to the forest floor.
A carpet of yellow and orange.
Wings ache for sun.

### Dance the way they do

January wept, thawed us all,
deceived us or coddled us—who
knows which? We needed something,
and January did what it could:
uncovered a lawn from December snows,
let rain pelt on shingles and drip
from swelling bud ends of birch.
Just when I thought
you were gone for good,
the air grew soft again,
starlings screed, shook out
their ordinary wings,
danced the way they do.
Funny how people scorn
these common birds, rejoicers
who keep the melody going,
keep it going when all else is dead
or frozen.

### Riding along beside

The other part of me
is riding
somewhere
off in the distance
in a willow break,
along a sunken creekbed,
halfway to the horizon.
You at my side.

We're heading back to camp.
The horses will graze.
There's nowhere to get to.

On foot to gather deadwood,
crouching to examine
a set of prints,
move on in silence,

Twilight.
Night.

We rekindle the fire
at dawn, whistle
to bring the mare close.
The other horses
follow her anywhere.

We take to the creek,
wend with it toward the cabin
at the edge of town.

Later, the city.

Indigo bunting in a date palm

### Song sparrow

The calendar says it's Washington's birthday.
There's no escaping the giant except
by looking up, out.

Sun's rising between Mr. MacKinnon's
and the corner house now; already
good progress in the shift to north,
though snow in the yard is waist-high.

This morning, blue, blue shadows
and distant crows en route
to open water or garbage tip;

and the lone song sparrow jumps forward,
pulls his whole body back, raking away
the snow on the feeding tray
to expose a few seeds. He's a persistent

small bundle of feathers, this his second
winter with me. Mornings I would rather
warm up, make coffee, look at the mail,

but I pull on socks and boots and scarf
and trudge through the drifts to sweep clean
the bird tray, leave more seeds.

*Pish-pish-pish*, I say, and the sparrow watches
from the middle of the bare weigela shrub.

The first walk of Sunday is from coffee pot
to pergola, then to window to watch
a little brown bird who seems to reside
deep inside me, but emerges daily into
my field of vision, as real as a heartbeat.

### Rental bees

The sun broke out today and the robin returned,
his song keen and consonant in April air.

Our mother used to play "The Robin's Return"
on the upright piano we inherited at one rental
behind an old inn, a house built in 1752.
The piano was not that old.

Neighbours and I know this robin,
saw him fledge, shooed away cats, cheered.

The sun brings old flies, huge, hairy,
from the attic to buzz at the windows.
Crocuses bloom along a south-facing foundation,
honeybees find them.

"Every honeybee fills with jealousy,"
Louis Armstrong sings,
"When they see you out with me.
"I don't blame them, goodness knows."

There was an article in the paper this week.
Honeybees have been disappearing. Lots of them.
Billions. Going off to die somewhere else
than near the hive. And worker bees
are forgetting to feed eggs and larvae.
A squash farmer is worried, says rental bees
will be hard to find this year.

Did we forget to sing "Honeysuckle Rose"
to guide bees home to the hive
when pollen has been gathered from far fields?

Who is playing "The Robin's Return" on an old upright?

### Red fox on the Blueshank Road

In a dream of hummingbirds,
I know if I close my eyes
I will be invisible.
If I slow the breath, move
among stalks of grass, part
the rough-stemmed tansy,
whisper *September,* pronounce
*breeze, early morning;*
if I forget my mammalian heart,
I can join their huddle.

There are seven of them,
wings folded, secrets
collected on silent feathers.
A male, ruby and emerald.
A female, grey-brown.
Two more pairs—males bright;
females, dun.
And here an unpaired female
turned towards me, searching
for her jewelled flash of mate,
listening for wings to hum the sky.

I close my eyes, lean into
the gathering of hummers.
I have practised for this,
have sought the cadence of stopped time
on languorous autumn afternoons
in meadows by the sea.

A disturbance of air thrills
the cilia of my right ear.
Rapid thrumming, whirring.
My heart quickens, remembers flight.

The lost male skims forward,
strums the moment, lands
beside his mate.
Eight, now. Eight winged beings,
paired, feather composed.
They are marking time with stillness.

I wake. Thrum and beat linger
beside my cheek, continue
into the day, humming beneath
my words and work, almost
disappearing, almost
disappearing me.

Later, an hour before sundown,
a fox crosses the road a distance
ahead of the car, hesitates
on the shoulder, crosses back.
I am close enough
to catch white-tipped tail,
black leggings.
Red fox on the Blueshank Road
lets me see she has been seen,
then slides into the alders.

I hear them all, now, there in the tangle
of goldenrod and crowfoot, there
in September tansy and squirrel-tail grass.
I hear them whirr and rustle, hear
how they begin the story again
and again.

## Weary

The world goes into its room
Shuts the door, weeps.
Out there, this afternoon,
all of it sad.

Go away. Leave the world alone
to remove dams, run rivers to sea,
return songbird to wolf willow,
wipe flies from children's faces,
make a fire and a pot of soup,
find the reed doll, feed the dogs.

Come back later, after the sky
has been filtered, ore unsmelted,
boreal forest regrown; elephants
easy in ancestral herds,
necessary sorrow sheltered in bones;
cetaceans swimming memory
up and down the oceans.
Birds to air.
Fish to sea.
Monkeys home with their families.

Go away.
A few moments, *please*.

*Gateleg Table,* by David Milne (1882-1953), oil on canvas
14" x 18"/35.6 x 45.7 cm, signed and dated top right by
David B. Milne, May 15, 1921.

### Gateleg table

Here at the table, after the great war,
before electricity hums every room,
only soundless melting in the icebox
to mark the second decade of the century.
Books from last night unshelved.
You, recalling it was in a letter to Theo
that Vincent said *mysterious vibrations
of kindred tones*, and then we remembered
Whitman's *voluptuous opiate shades*—I fled
to squeeze words onto the already scraped
and put-away palette: cobalt blue,
violet, sun, moon—returned to see
your sweet head bowed to angle of entry.

The pond holds the sky on a blue afternoon.
Sedges spike the shallow water, drenched
in longing to disperse as clouds—drift,
disappear. You stir and look up, unfurl.

There is nothing I can paint to utter you,
so I choose a field where you saw a neighbour
shimmer as sun and horse finished for the day.
I looked only when I heard your small gasp,
a certain intake that pivots the cosmos
and flings it into my lap.
At the end of a furrow
the horse turned toward home,
to stall and scented hay,
the man home to steam rising,
a lid lifted to check potatoes.
The weary ones rest. Soon another war
will shake the century into, out of, towards—

This evening, a long lavender dusk is enough.
We'll light the wall lamp after a bit,
clear the books away, make supper, talk.
Later, children will admire the finger-waves
of your bobbed hair and the sweep of your skirt.
"Oh, Mama!" they'll say. "Mama, you were so young!"
They will run their fingers along the edge
of the table, play with the turned gateleg
that transformed our daily ritual of ordinary
into cave, fort, secret.
One of them will sit as you do now, composed
to a sonnet of stillness, reading perfection
with a slow, blue, purple sigh.

## Straw between the rows

Along the shore
and up across a gentle slope,
strawberry plants hug the clay,
suck up sun,
soon to burst
into fruit—red
sweet stain on your lips,
your fingers.
The straw between the rows
warm, fragrant.

You could lie here:
breathe in last summer;
exhale into autumn and blue days;
oats and barley winnowed, stored;
chaff on the berries
before the snow flies;

You could lie down
between the red rows,
let your bones soak up the sun.
Throw an arm over your eyes.

Listen:
in the hedgerow,
sparrow and bee.

You could stop
right here,
stretch out
like a cat.

## Abandoned tracks

Queen Anne's lace, brown and ragged.
Everywhere, scatterings of seed threshed
by wind on a floor of hard snow—
tansy, sow thistle, yarrow.
Afternoon slant of sun on stubble
reminds the sky of a certain blue.
Still-green mullein thaws, freezes again.
The same three wild apples dangle
on a perfect tree by the railroad tracks.
And where the wind has uncovered them
by a fence, ferns stand, umber and present.
Wild roses spike above the drifts, rosehips
blood on a white sheet. And over there,
clumps of burdocks pray for long-haired dogs.

### This is a dream or war with Iraq

Mrs. MacKinnon called, nervous,
"The fence is falling down," she says,
"A new one...before winter?"
"Is it customary," I ask,
"for neighbours to share the cost
of a shared fence?"
She sighs, relieved.
She does not have to explain;
she has never travelled to foreign
countries, knows language with strangers
only for accidents—a husband
felled by a stroke, too heavy
to lift from the front stair.

Mrs. MacKinnon has
put
up
a
chain-
link
fence
where turned posts
were planted
by her husband.
He was young once, like the spruce
boards of the fence,
oozing sap.
She has been a widow long enough
to have hung curtains
between then and now.
She hires young men to rake
leaves, build a fence,
cut the patch of grass
where the old vegetable garden lay
A jar of pickles,
her mother-in-law's recipe, waits
on a shelf in the cellar.

I am raking leaves
by Mrs. MacKinnon's
chain-
link
fence.

It is a soft, overcast day.
How quickly tansy, nightshade,
young maples will make a solid
hedge again: this the thought as
I kneel, hands crumbling dark earth.

In July I moved the woodpile.
A tan and green frog escaped,
surprised, tumbled by hardwood blocks,
home caved in, hurt.
I caught it in work gloves,
saw it would heal, carried it
to the jungle along Mrs. MacKinnon's
old board fence.

Slowly, then, I unbuilt
the tumbled woodpile,
two cords,
eight more tan and green frogs,
eight gloved resettlements.

I am on my knees,
hands crumbling moist earth,
the day is soft, overcast—
And I remember:
I must pick up the children!
It is late, school will be over!

And now I am in the school, searching
for my children
I open my mouth to speak,
to call them, and
there is an explosion, felt and heard.

I am thrown and throw
myself to the floor.
My right eardrum bursts—
a cartoon drawing, torn edges
where a rock has pierced paper.

I calculate what has happened,
what can be done to restore this ear
to normal. All these things happen
at once—the explosion,

the roof open to the dome of sky,
the sky filled with reds, whites, heats,
my hand holding together the back of my ear.

A bone pokes through the right side
of my temple. "This is it," I think,
words slow as punctuation.

And then survival spreads sure,
a wave washes every cell.
Everyone has been thrown
to the floor, everyone
has burst open in small places.
I know about exits and stampedes,
know about moving quickly.

Here on a drafting table
is a blueprint of intelligence
overlaid with a map of experience—
this is the way to enter,
this is where to leave,
here is pain, and over here
is death.

For a moment the air thickens,
darkens, swirls,
shimmering and black.
But awareness is undamaged.

Everywhere is perfect calm,
perfect hearing.
And everywhere are images unchanged:
  Forests with birds.
  Back yards with children.
  A patch of snow.
  Mayflowers.

I lie holding my body together,
my cheek against the earth
as though it were our old dog—
a golden stray, fourteen years together,
her sweet glide into death in my arms—
and before this dream ends
I have time enough
to say good-bye.

### I am the road

I am the road, the red road.
I muddy your hem, the weight
of your long skirts weightier.
You hurry, the child is sick.

I am the road through wilderness,
your lifeline, the letter home,
news from the old country.

I am the road the horse knows
by heart, clop-clopping,
a lazy night home
or a too-fast gallop
to the neighbour's cabin,
and back, faster, in time.

I am the red road,
the sucking-hoof mud road
in April, October, January thaw.

I am the red road, and before this,
the corduroy road, a swath
the length of a shortcut—trees
felled, logs sideways, rolled
trunk against trunk, lying close,
nestled or spiked in red clay,
all the way from port to settlement.

I am the bowered road songbirds found:
sing, mate, nest, hatch, gone.

I am the red road, and before corduroy-logs,
I was a path through never-cut pine,
beech, red oak. I was clay on sandstone,
pressed, uplifted—fissure, bone,
shell, red mudstone, green.

I am the road that dips to the hollow
where tree frogs claim the sky in spring.
I am the straightaway by a field—
the house was there, the barn against that
northline of spruce. See, the apple trees
never forget; bees help them remember.

Humans come, mostly go. Their presence
indelible, ink scritched on vellum or
spilled, making a mess of things. Middens
of muffler, chassis, disc, and harrow.

I am the red road, the cricket road,
the fox-and-crow, red-squirrel-alarm,
flock-swooping-August-swirling-blackbird road.

I am the ghost road, the partings sudden
or sorrowful—mist at the bottom of the hill.
Feel the chill as you pass through?
They can't stop saying good-bye.

I am the sleigh track in winter,
the road to church, to town,
graveyard, ceilidh, wedding,
railway station, ferry.

I am the road.
I am the red road home.

### *Almost always the same*

The shovel slides neatly down along the edge
of the old border, mourning dove nearby, shards
unearthed, sometimes delft with a tracery of blue.

Almost always, the same small trapezoid
brings me to my knees among upturned sods
and scylla, bulbs small as wild camas root

we found along the Milk River,
tent pitched in riparian shade,
cottonwood fluff everywhere, summer snow.

I used to save them in a jar,
broken collection on a windowsill.
Now I leave the bits of china
to gentle turnings with primrose and
crocus finding spring passage to the sky;
leave them in easy earth under May's steady rain
and in sun-baked density of July.

### No more than that

I have sat at enough cafés,
flown into passing houses from train windows,
tracked a glance from the next car at a stoplight,
drifted into ten thousand lives
at airports and bus stations,
watched, felt the heart stir, followed,
until a life passing by—
a certain entry through the eyes,
the curve of lip, a hand on a counter—
is no more than that.

I saw an indigo bunting in a date palm.

## Acknowledgements

Thanks to Cole Cantin for permission to use his phrase, "afternoon horses," for the title of this collection, and to both Chase Cantin and Cole Cantin for permission to publish poems about them.

My hearty thanks to editor Gillian Robinson and to Libby Oughton and Melissa Carroll for early reading of manuscript.

Thanks to Cecily Donnelly for permission to use her painting *Fireweed Trail* on the cover of the book and for digging out the photographs of us as children on horseback.

The lines *"Yo escribí cinco versos:/uno verde,/otro era un pan redondo..."* quoted from Pablo Neruda's "Oda a la crítica," translated by Margaret Sayers Peden in *The Poetry of Pablo Neruda*, NY: Farrar, Strauss and Giroux, 2003, p. 382.

The long poem, "Subtracting by seventeen," first appeared in September 2006, in Saturday Morning Chapbooks series 3, *Subtracting by Seventeen and other poems,* edited by David Helwig, Joseph Sherman, and Hugh MacDonald.

"Gateleg table" was first published by the Confederation Centre of the Arts in a catalogue to accompany the June-to-September 2003 exhibition of the poem, part of the *Writing ON the Wall* series, curated by Joseph Sherman. The poem is a response to *Gateleg Table,* by David Milne (1882–1953), oil on canvas 14" x 18"/35.6 x 45.7 cm, signed and dated top right by David B. Milne, May 15, 1921.

"Red fox on the Blue Shank Road" was first published in *Landmarks: An Anthology of New Atlantic Canadian Poetry of the Land*, edited by Brent MacLaine and Hugh MacDonald, Acorn Press, 2001.

"No more than that" was first published in *The New Poets of Prince Edward Island*, Ragweed Press, 1991.

"I am the road" was commissioned by CBC Radio for regional network broadcast August 5, 2002. PEI Poet Laureate John Smith and I each wrote a poem entitled "I am the road," and interwove them in performance for broadcast.

"Honeysuckle Rose": lyrics and music by Louis Armstrong, page 63.